KT-468-961

CONTENTS

INTRODUCTION

"By nominating this a year of Public Sculpture we want to pay tribute to the sculptural inheritance which previous generations have seen fit to bestow upon us and encourage everyone to look around and enjoy it!" -

(Sir Jocelyn Stevens, English Heritage).

The year 2000 brought good news for sculpture and for us, the public. Public Sculpture was chosen by English Heritage as its Millennium theme because sculpture has always been the commemorative art form. Luckily, at the same time, sculpture in general is in the ascendant.

We, the public, are the beneficiaries, and judge and jury of sculptures intended for us, many of which are publicly owned. Statues and monuments enhance public places, lifting our eyes and hearts.

To launch the themed year, English Heritage published a 'Users Guide to Public Sculpture' and asked the PMSA (Public Monuments and Sculpture Association), of which I am a member, to supply the writing.

In order to prepare the East of England section, which centred on Norwich, I started looking at sculptures and arranged a sculpture trail of ten works in the city. On publication day, 15th March, the trail was illustrated in the Eastern Daily Press. The newspaper was very helpful and willing to support the idea of my carrying on with the task of looking at Norfolk's sculpture. These were to be printed as individual features which were accompanied by a photograph.

The outcome is in these pages and once assembled, the features lend an impression of being a collection. In fact, the different works were assembled over centuries and are only bound together by location in one English county. Norfolk's 'collection' is unique but not unusual in England. It is small compared to those of Liverpool or Birmingham, where complete records of Public Sculpture have been published by Liverpool University Press in conjunction with the National Recording Project and The Royal Commission of Historic Monuments in England.

What do we see in Norfolk? Whatever remained of Iceni, Roman or Saxon sculptural work must have disappeared by Norman times, from when such work came into the churches and cathedral. The material was stone, imported to this area. But, by late Mediaeval and Tudor times, masons were providing memorials for the rich and worthy using alabaster and, later, Italian marble. By the 17th century, non-ecclesiastical buildings were embellished with statues, such as the figure of Charles II on the Custom House at King's Lynn. The architect had been on the Grand Tour of Europe, seeing ruins of ancient civilisations. The Stuarts turned to Classicism, aided by foreign exiles who were skilled sculptors.

From such times, statues emerged onto the street. By the 19th century commemoration was fashionable and at its peak. Sculptors were trained at the R.A schools and became famous. The county acquired some status as the birthplace of Nelson, and its pillar preceded that in London's Trafalgar Square. Norwich did not attract many municipal statues of politicians and manufacturers, as the prospering municipalities up North had done.

On the other hand, Norfolk could rise to the occasion, as with the Leicester Monument. It was on a large scale and involved many meetings and disputes, but it was paid for by public subscription and its unveiling was witnessed by a crowd of 10,000.

By the time Queen Victoria died, society had begun to tire of the impassive statues of the great and good. A group of artists, the Vorticists, said they would do anything to replace the endless 'weeping whiskers', a reference to Sir J. Boehm, sculptor of many royal persons. Their arguments were a part of the general reaction to what was seen as pompous anachronism in the statues of dignitaries, although, as stated, Norfolk's list does not include any of these.

In the midst of the debate over style, the 20th century brought war and subsequent memorials to the fallen. Two noted here are the extravagant and beautiful Boer War Memorial in Norwich and the untriumphal figure of a dead soldier in Ditchingham by F. Derwent Wood. However, the conflict over style did not disappear.

From around 1950 onwards, there was a general shift in public sculpture, away from the authoritative yet unselfconscious commemoration of a subject, towards the expressive stance, which insists that what matters is the artistic quality of the object. There has always been a risk of the public not liking a work of art and these newer works do not necessarily reflect a culture that is comfortable with itself.

Equally, a sculpture can take a while to make itself at home, as with the polished bronze shapes by Bernard Meadows, which were sited on the front of The EDP's own building. Opinions were mixed on the arrival of his untitled work in 1969, but after about fifteen years it has become an accepted feature of the city. During the same period, with growing interest in leisure, tourism and heritage, traditional sculptures have come to be seen in a different light. We now wish to conserve and maintain our historical monuments. Norfolk's pieces need conservation, notably the Norfolk Pillar in Great Yarmouth, which is to be further repaired after being fenced off for years with warnings about falling stonework. Another in danger is the terracotta 'Armed Science' by John Bell in the city cemetry. The East wind does the damage.

While making a survey of public sculpture, I soon started to bend the rules by including memorials in churches. In a sense I do regard them as public, though many will disagree and I can see why. One motive was to bolster the list with big names like Scheemakers, Westmacott and Flaxman, Derwent Wood and G.F Watts.

Church memorials were certainly intended for the public and those in the Cathedral are open to view at most hours. What is shown in these pages are only a small proportion of the vast wealth of Norfolk's church memorials. There is much more hidden away, not only the grand works of men like Caius Cibber, whose 1672 monument to Judge Spelman stands in Narborough, but numerous works of Norwich masons like Robert Page, John de Carle and Thomas Rawlins.

Also outside the true definition of public sculpture, and not included in this book, are the fine works inside galleries and stately houses. Norwich's Castle Museum has works by Bell, Gibson, Paolozzi, Henry Moore and Bernard Meadows. Holkham Hall contains 18th and 19th century works by Nollekens and Boehm. But it was the arrival of the Sainsbury Collection in 1973 which put Norwich on the international gallery circuit. Side by side with ancient carvings and miniatures are 20th century works by Moore, Giacometti, Richier, Arp, MacWilliam, Epstein and others. There too is Degas' famous 'Little Dancer'.

Very few of the truly public sculptures have been lost, though Norwich was bombed in the war. The statue on Norwich's old Hippodrome disappeared. Other pieces, such as J.Boehm's 'Mother & Child' and the Cavell Monument, were moved to allow more and more cars. The county has no village sculpture or public fountains and there are towns with no sculpture at all, although Norfolk has exceptional village signs. These are mostly in wood, which is not really a sculptural medium.

Others would argue that it is, in which case the contemporary carvings of Mark Goldsworthy in North Walsham, Holt and Homersfield should be noted. Like a large oak totem pole, his carving in Norwich's Chapelfield Gardens commemorates the 1999 quadcentenary of Will Kemp and his fellow actors who danced all the way from London. It was commissioned by Norfolk Contemporary Art Society. The city of Norwich should be grateful to NCAS as many of the sculptures that have recently taken their place in Norwich were commissioned by them. In addition to sculptures shown in this book, such as Liliane Lijn's 'Extrapolation' and Jonathan Clarke's 'Daedalus', the society raised works by Bernard Reynolds, George Fullard and others.

Comparing sculptures and assessing Norfolk's 'collection' can only be done by looking at pictures of all the works together. Then we see, for example, that the largest bronze figure is Edward VII, and that the only equestrian statue is the Maharajah's in Thetford. We can also see that, overall, there has been relatively little new sculpture, considering how much development has taken place.

An opportunity missed today, is the old practice of raising money for sculpture by public subscriptions. The support of architects, planners and patrons is essential. Too many controls result in blandness and too few can allow badly located or unsuitable sculpture. However, if the current high status of sculpture endures, then Norfolk might provide locations which excite sculptors.

A real objective in this survey and book is to play a useful part in future considerations. We need to have some idea of what we would like to see instated – and where? An abstract perhaps? A fountain maybe, since we have none. Why not a statue of a shoemaker or the last agricultural worker? If it's regional identity we are after, what about Boadicea in her war chariot heading for London, or a poet, or John Cotman?

By looking at what Norfolk has already, we may get some ideas for public sculptures in the future.

Richard Barnes. Autumn 2001.

In St. Mary's in Tittleshall you can stand in one spot and see four grand memorials in marble from the 19th, 18th, 17th and even 16th centuries, almost a lesson in history, with works by Nicholas Stone, Roubilliac and Nollekens. All are to the Coke family and the oldest tells a personal history. This is the memorial to Bridget, wife of Edward Coke, whose later monument stands alongside. One of the Paston family, she was 33 years old when she died in 1598. The pink and cream alabaster memorial is about ten feet tall, with the family crest above, and presents her as an Elizabethan lady kneeling before a dark tablet within an arched recess. The columns on either side are decorated with carved and painted ribbons, flames, fruits and two books – one open, the other closed. In a line below are eight of Bridget's ten children, their heads shiny with curls.

These monuments in alabaster, a crystalline gypsum found in the Midlands, were typical of an earlier period and usually featured reclining effigies. Bridget's memorial probably came from masons' workshops in Southwark. Although the sculptor cannot be named, he would have been the best available. Her husband, eulogised in the inscription of the adjacent memorial as 'High Priest of Persuasion, the Soul of Law and Revealer of its Secrets', wielded very considerable power as Chief Justice under Elizabeth I and James I. Nationally important, all four Tittleshall monuments need minor repairs, for which the village church is seeking assistance.

MEMORIAL TO BRIDGET, WIFE OF
EDWARD COKE
1598, SCULPTOR UNKNOWN
TITTLESHALL CHURCH

A statue of King Charles II embellishes the outside of the Custom House in Kings Lynn. Originally the 1683 merchants' exchange for the port of Lynn Regis, this is rightly considered to be one of the most perfect buildings in all Europe and it is easy to imagine ships' captains sailing extra miles to trade in such splendour. It was surveyed, designed and overseen by the artistic and scholarly architect, Henry Bell, 1647-1711, who was educated locally and at Cambridge, then along the Grand Tour of Europe. A landed merchant and later mayor, he was also a friend of Sir John Turner, who financed this and other public works.

There is every reason to think that Henry Bell, who was extremely talented as a painter and engraver, would himself have guided the sculptor or mason. He attended every detail in the elaborate design of the beautiful building, including the niche and statue of the restored and popular king, correct in every detail of his garter robes. Close by are the heads of Commerce, Ceres and Bacchus, emblems of this port's trade, all carved in the same Ketton stone. The king's bronze sceptre was recently replaced and the building extensively conserved. Now in the hands of the Borough Council and looking resplendent, it was reopened in 1999 by HRH Charles, Prince of Wales.

1683 STATUE OF KING CHARLES II
DESIGNED BY HENRY BELL
THE CUSTOM HOUSE, KING'S LYNN.

The mortuary chapel of the Hare family at Stow Bardolph church near Downham Market is famous for its rare and remarkable 1743 wax effigy of Sarah Hare. But, for those who look at sculpture, the numerous grand marble memorials to other members of the ancient family are of greater consequence. One of the finest is the earlier monument to Susanna Hare, 1684-1741, signed by the esteemed sculptor, Peter Scheemakers. Raised by her brother Thomas, it towers 15 feet and only just fits inside the roof structure. Above a large inscribed base, Susanna reclines on a bier, raising her half-veiled head. Above her, set against grey marble, two cherubs' faces peer from white clouds and, still higher, a classical frieze is emblazoned with her crest. The latin inscription tells of her simple truth, noted constancy and excellent gentleness.

This is Peter Scheemakers' only work in Norfolk. His father, brother and son were all sculptors. Born in Antwerp in 1691, he walked all the way to Italy to study in Rome. He was active for 45 years in England and established himself as a leading sculptor of classical figures, architectural features and prestigious memorials, including 13 statues in Westminster Abbey. This figure of Susanna Hare is quite similar to those in memorials by his brother Henry and his rival, Michael Rysbrack.

1741 MONUMENT TO SUSANNA HARE
BY PETER SCHEEMAKERS
STOW BARDOLPH,
NR. DOWNHAM MARKET

At one time prisoners were kept below Bungay's 1689 Buttercross in a cage before attending the nearby magistrates court. In 1754 the elegant octagonal structure was surmounted by a lead-covered figure of 'Justice'. Pevsner suggests that this may be the work of Henry Cheere, 1703-1781, who, with his brother John, worked from a yard in Westminster in marble, stone, bronze and lead. Between them, the brothers supplied figures for Oxford, Westminster Abbey, The Bank of England and Stourhead. They also took over the stock of the deceased sculptor, John Nost.

So, even if Pevsner is right in attributing this statue to Cheere, none can be sure who actually made the Bungay statue; or even if she was actually intended as 'Justice', since the figure looks more like Ceres or a Gainsborough lady, and may have had a different purpose. However, with the additions to either hand of a sword and a pair of scales in metal, she serves as a graceful emblem of justice, not only one of the most attractive, but one of the very few in England without a blindfold. Swaffham has a statue of Ceres in the market place and Thetford has a Coade figure of Justice on its Guildhall, but this statue, only a few yards out of Norfolk, is unlike either of them.

1754 JUSTICE
ATTRIBUTED BY PEVSNER TO HENRY CHEERE
BUNGAY, SUFFOLK

1794 Pyramid and Hobart Mausoleum
by Joseph Bonomi,
Great Wood, Blickling

The finest pyramid in Norfolk is in a clearing in Great Wood behind Blickling Hall. At first sight, it is impressive, 45 ft tall on a 45 ft square base, with smooth, grey, stone-clad sides. There are classical doorways in each face and the inscribed West door is topped by a heraldic bull. Erected by his wife, this is the mausoleum of John Hobart, 2nd Earl of Buckingham, who died in 1793. It was designed by Joseph Bonomi, 1739-1808, an Italian architect who had been invited by Robert Adam to England, where he provided numerous Neo-classical interiors. His source for the Norfolk pyramid was the tomb of Caius Cestrius in Rome.

However, his son, Joseph Bonomi junior, was a sculptor and he looked to Egypt itself. Born in 1796, while the pyramid was being built, he lived in London, attending the Academy Schools and working under Joseph Nollekens. Then, aged 28, Bonomi left for Egypt, where for twenty years he drew antiquities and joined explorations. Returning to England, he designed the Egyptian Court of the Crystal Palace and later curated the Soane Museum. Father and son, the Bonomis were an influential part of the interest in Ancient Egyptian monuments. There are obelisks and sphinxes in North Norfolk, and all over England.

1802 MEMORIAL TO WILLIAM COWPER
BY JOHN FLAXMAN
DEREHAM

The memorial to William Cowper, 1731-1800, carved in marble by one of England's finest sculptors, is in St Nicholas's Church in Dereham. Cowper was a popular poet and translator who suffered from depression and mental instability. His finer works, 'The Task' and 'Olney Hymns', were completed before his arrival in Norfolk in 1795 with his elderly friend, Mary Unwin, who kept house and looked after him. Above an inscription by the writer's friend and biographer, William Hayley, the simple memorial shows a leafy frond curling gracefully over a bulky bible, which stands on a shelf. A second, smaller book leans towards it: it is 'The Task'.

The sculptor and illustrator, John Flaxman, 1755-1826, was famous in his lifetime, far more so than his friend, William Blake. With a classical touch and a visionary's imagination, his genius was recognised at an early age and he later became Professor of Sculpture at the Royal Academy with commissions for monuments and statues throughout England. There are at least two other memorials in Norfolk by Flaxman, one of which was raised in 1803 to Rev E. Nelson, the Admiral's father, in Burnham Thorpe.

An elegant marble relief of a beautiful woman is set against the wall in Ketteringham Church. She kneels in grief over a helmet, halberd and sheathed sword. Behind her, set against the 6 feet tall, grey marble tablet is a stylised and symbolic tree of life. Erected in 1807 by Charlotte Atkyns for her husband, Edward Atkyns of Ketteringham Hall, who died in 1794, and their son, a cavalry officer, who died ten years later, the memorial tells of the father's 'unsullied integrity' and the son's 'highly cultivated mind and polished manners'. The mourner might be seen as Charlotte herself. A London actress, she married Edward Atkyns and lived in France, befriending Marie Antoinette during the Revolution. She was a role model for The Pimpernel, making several attempts to rescue the imprisoned Queen and, later, the dauphin. She died in poverty in Paris.

Sir Richard Westmacott, 1775-1856, was the father and son of sculptors named Richard. He was the most successful, studying in Rome under Canova, before returning to establish his business in London. He became Professor of Sculpture in the. Academy schools and was knighted in 1837. His most famous sculptures are 'Achilles' at Hyde Park Corner and the pediment figures fronting the British Museum. His commissions exceed 300 works, including three others in Norfolk.

1807. Memorial to Edward Atkyns by Sir Richard Westmacott Ketteringham Church

1819. The Norfolk Pillar   EDP. 1962
Architect: William Wilkins. Original statuary: 1817 Coade of Lambeth
Great Yarmouth

The 141 feet tall Nelson Monument, known as The Norfolk Pillar, seen from afar in Great
Yarmouth, was the work of the Norfolk architect, William Wilkins. It was raised by public
subscription in 1819, more than twenty years before the column and statue in Trafalgar Square.
Inside the fluted doric column of Mansfield stone is a staircase, something the London
monument, a fraction taller, does not possess. The base is carved with wreaths, the names of the
great hero's sea battles, and a rousing inscription: NELSON, BY BIRTH, LINEAGE AND
EDUCATION. BY MIND, BY MANNERS AND BY DISPOSITION, NORFOLK PROUDLY BOASTS
HER OWN.

Up the pillar, a surround of six identitical figures of 'Victory' form a podium which supports the
heroic statue of Britannia. Surveying all, with trident in her outstretched arm, she gazes inland,
rather than out to sea. The original statues were made of artificial stone by Coade of Lambeth,
who employed a number of modellers. The Coade stone figures deteriorated and were replaced
by concrete copies in 1896 which also fell into disrepair, leading to concerns for safety. It was
decided in 1982 that all the statues should be replaced with fibre-glass replicas, surface etched
to a suitable texture. Although the site is currently closed, with warnings about falling masonry,
the extensive conservation and regular maintenance work, funded by a number of sources, has
ensured the survival of a monument of national importance.

1845. 'IRRIGATION'. SOUTH-FACING FRIEZE, LEICESTER MONUMENT BY JOHN HENNING JUNIOR HOLKHAM PARK

From Holkham Hall, one sees the 125 ft Corinthian column crowned by a sheaf of wheat, known as the Leicester Monument. It is England's finest memorial to the greatness of farming, raised in honour of Thomas Coke, Earl of Leicester, the famous Norfolk agrarian improver and politician, who died in 1842. Designed by W. Donthorn and built between 1845 and 1850 by J. Watson's Norwich stonemasonry firm, it was publicly subscribed by Coke's tenants and admirers. They collected £4,000 and voted that it should be in Holkham, rather than Norwich. A walk through the wooded park is rewarded by a view of the features. A plough, a group of Southdown sheep, a Devon ox and a seed drill, all lifesize in stone, sit at each corner. The sculptor of the livestock, which are exceptional, is not known.

Between these are 18ft wide panels, one inscribed and three showing scenes from Coke's life. The South panel, where two central figures stand with their horses, is well composed and the stone least eroded. Here is Coke, conversing with the Duke of Bedford. The topic is Irrigation. The geologist, 'Strata' Smith, is nearby, his foreman wearing a farmer's smock. These bas-reliefs were by John Henning Jr, 1802-1857, who assisted his father for many years and provided busts at Woburn and Windsor. His work was chiefly in reliefs, notably classical figures on Decimus Burton's triple screen at Hyde Park Corner. § *see notes page 46*

Within the image: William Schomberg Robert 2ᵈ Marquis of Lothian, born 12ᵗʰ August 1832, died 4ᵗʰ July 1870

1878. MEMORIAL TO THE MARQUIS OF LOTHIAN
BY G. F WATTS, BLICKLING CHURCH

When the owner of Blickling Hall, William Robert, 8th Marquis of Lothian, died at the age of 38 in 1870, his wife, Constance, commissioned a memorial from a remarkable artist who had been a friend of theirs. The marble monument was erected in 1878 in the aisle of Blickling church. Two human-lifesize female angels stand at either end of the carved marble bed, upon which lies the handsome figure of the dead Marquis. The detail is the finest, not only on the beard and hair of the figure of Lothian, but on the cut-in creases and furls of drapery covering him. Through all this, a great veined shake in the marble spreads rust-red streaks towards the winged spirits. Among all the angels or chimera ever carved, these would stand out. They are freestanding, beautiful and, if such a thing can be said of angels with huge wings, 'realistic'.

George Frederick Watts, 1817-1904, was a very successful painter of the Aesthetic Movement who proved that he was a sculptor too. He extended the reach of the medium with new techniques of simulating cloth, cutting in marble in a way that was unequalled, as in the Blickling group. As well as memorials and ideal works, he made larger bronzes, including a statue of the poet, Tennyson, at Lincoln, and his famous equestrian work, 'Physical Energy', in Kensington Gardens. For some years Watts had visited Blickling, witnessing the progress of the nobleman's mysterious disease, and had painted 'Love and Death' with an image of the Marchioness warding off the illness. She too is remembered in a nearby marble relief with three angels by A. G. Walker, 1901. But the most tangible legacy of the Lothian family, whose crest features an angel, is Blickling Hall itself, which the 11th Marquis bequeathed to the National Trust in 1940.

The figure of King Edward VII is seen outside the school which bears his name; with Charles Ist & 2nd in the town centre, this is King's Lynn's third statue of a monarch. Unveiled in 1906 by his wife, Queen Alexandria, it is a pleasant image of the popular king in the middle of his reign. After 60 years as Prince of Wales, King Edward was a sociable and cultivated man with close relations in Europe's royal families who spoke five languages and was well informed on foreign affairs. The almost twice lifesize, bronze statue shows him sitting comfortably on an elaborately crowned chair, with his great robe of state loosely about him, a dignified and somewhat slender figure dressed in academic and coronation attire, including a stylish cap. To complete the surprisingly informal, yet traditional, appearance, a pair of cherubs play behind the King's head. The sculpture and the school buildings were paid for by J. Lancaster, a former pupil.

The sculptor, William Robert Colton, 1867-1921, was highly thought of at the turn of the last century. He studied and later taught sculpture at the Royal Academy schools, making classical statuettes including 'The Wavelet' in the Tate Gallery. He received commissions for portrait busts and public monuments, notably part of the Royal Artillery Memorial, close to Hyde Park Corner. He was later elected R.A and President of Royal Society of British Sculptors.

1906. King Edward VII
by W. R Colton
King Edward VII School, King's Lynn

**1920 SOLDIER'S MEMORIAL
BY FRANCIS DERWENT WOOD R.A
DITCHINGHAM CHURCH**

It was a surprise to find this, one of the finest 20th century war memorials I have seen, in a Norfolk village. Against the wall inside Ditchingham church is a wide expanse of highly polished black marble, inscribed with thirty local names and roman numerals for 1914-1919. The realistic bronze figure of a soldier in greatcoat and battledress lies on the smooth slab, as if outside a field hospital. His handsome features in repose, the soldier's head is pillowed on an army pack; above his boots, mud-caked bindings recall trench conditions. Unconventional yet tasteful, the superb memorial conveys a mood of darkness and rest. It was commissioned and unveiled in 1920 by William Carr of Ditchingham Hall at a cost of £1,100, with a contribution from Rider Haggard and the families of the dead. Five names were added after the 2nd World War.

Francis Derwent Wood, 1871-1926, was a very accomplished sculptor of the period. After study in Paris, he became modelling master at Glasgow School of Art. He provided sculpture for Glasgow and London, including part of the Victoria Memorial and 'Nude', a female figure on Chelsea Embankment. While at work on the soldier, the sculptor had another Norfolk order, this being the marble memorial to Violet Morgan in Norwich Cathedral.

'ONE OF THE BRAVEST MEN THAT EVER LIVED'. In front of the Cromer council offices on East Cliff is a paved recess where the heroic lifeboatman, Henry Blogg, 1876-1954, is commemorated. The realistic bust by the sculptor, James Woodford, shows Blogg in sowester and oilskins, his strong features in repose, as if staring at the horizon. Beneath, on a stone plinth is a plaque with an inscription recording his gallantry as coxwain of Cromer lifeboats from 1909-1947, winning 3 gold and 4 silver medals for gallantry.

The bust was presented anonymously by a Miss E. Scales, whose identity remained a secret until her death. A visitor to the town, she and her sister had deplored the lack of a memorial to the former coxwain, who, with his crew, had rescued a total of 873 lives in 53 years. The sculptor, James Woodford, 1893-1976, was at Nottingham Art College before the Great War, and afterwards at the Royal College of Art. He made the 1953 'Queen's Beasts' in Westminster Abbey and the WW2 memorial in front of the British Medical Association building in London. His sculpture of the lifeboatman was gratefully received in Cromer and a wreath was laid by the new coxwain, Henry Davies, at the unveiling in 1962. Nowadays, Blogg is doubly honoured, because the bronze bust was replaced in 1999 with a cast-alloy replica and the original was moved to the new boathouse at the end of the pier.

1962. HENRY BLOGG, COXWAIN
BY JAMES WOODFORD R.A
CROMER

Great political thinker or republican traitor? It is impossible to leave politics aside when looking at the gilded bronze statue of Thomas Paine, 1737-1809, in Thetford's King Street. Over-lifesize, he stands on an inscribed stone base, a muscular figure in period dress, who clutches a book and points a pen towards America. Tom Paine was born and educated in the town, becoming an excise collector and subsequently a radical writer. His 1775 'Common Sense' and 'The Crisis' enflamed the Independence movement in America, while his most famous work, 'The Rights of Man', 1791, propped the principles of the French Revolution. He lived in exile in both countries and, while in France, wrote 'The Age of Reason' and apparently helped Napoleon plan the invasion of England.

It is sometimes said that authorities in Thetford in 1964 were slow to appreciate the need for a monument. The fact is they were urged to accept the gift of the statue by the Tom Paine Foundation of New York. The choice of the sculptor, Charles Wheeler, 1892-1974, could not be criticised. Wheeler was President of the Royal Academy, with works in the Tate Gallery, and was honoured for services to Sculpture and eventually knighted. His dynamic and powerful figure of Paine is perhaps an overstatement in the ancient street. It is one of only a few statues in England raised by foreign request.

§ *see notes page 46*

1964. THOMAS PAINE
BY SIR CHARLES WHEELER R.A
THETFORD

At Butten Island on the river in Thetford is the equestrian statue of Prince Duleep Singh, 1838-1893, last Maharajah of the old Sikh empire of the Punjab, centred on Lahore, now in Pakistan. Lifesize in bronze, he is a watchful, experienced rider on a spirited arab horse, his left hand resting on a sheathed sword. He wears a fine coat and jewelled turban and sunlight catches details in the stirrups and brocaded bridle. A polished plinth bears the Sikh emblem, crests and two inscriptions painted in gold, one facing East in Gurmukhi, a Sanskrit derivative, the other in English. It explains how the Punjab was annexed in 1849 after the second Anglo-Sikh war. Treasures, including the revered Koh-i-noor diamond, were removed and the boy Maharajah brought to England, finally to Elveden Hall, four miles from Thetford. Queen Victoria felt quite maternal towards him and he remained with his family, rebuilding Elveden in the process. After about 1884, realising the true consequences of his exile, Duleep Singh planned to return to the Punjab. He re-embraced Sikhism and set off to Europe, to be watched by spies until his death in Paris. His memorial is significant and confers a freedom denied in life.

The sculptor, Denise Dutton, was born in 1964, and studied at the the Sir Henry Doulton School of Sculpture, and developed an affinity and skill with lifesize equine statuary, a task beyond some sculptors. When one of her exhibits was seen by the Maharajah Duleep Singh Centenary Trust, the commission for Norfolk's only equestrian work followed. Thousands of Sikhs arrived to witness its arrival in the town a year before the ceremonial unveiling by HRH The Prince of Wales in 1999.

1998. MAHARAJAH DULEEP SINGH.
BY DENISE DUTTON
THETFORD

**1998. BERGH APTON SIGN
BY KEITH BAILEY**

Sited by Bussey Bridge on the river Chet at the southern edge of Bergh Apton, is an impressive sculpture in Portland stone, of hybrid appearance somewhere between village sign and ancient megalith, or mark stone. It was one of three sculptures commissioned by trustees of the extremely successful Bergh Apton Sculpture Trail, which took place 1997-1999. The village name is carved in Teutonic script beneath a zoomorphic symbol, a semi-realistic horned bull. The outline was copied from an artifact found by archaeologists in a Saxon settlement near the prominent hill where the church stands. Astonishingly, the stone was placed initially on the Brooke road in 1998, but was moved after a single voice claimed that it showed a heathen image within view of the church!

The sculptor, Keith Bailey, was born in 1929 and spent 5 years in art college followed by National Conscription. Based in Cambridge, his first job was to assist in the stone carving in the American War Cemetery at Madingley. His work is chiefly in lettering, heraldic and architectural stone carving in the university, notably at Downing College. Most recently, in 2000, his carved and lettered columns commemorating two former students, Benjamin Britten and WH Auden, were unveiled at Greshams School in Norfolk.

The bronze statue of the famous naval explorer, George Vancouver, 1758-1798, stands on the old quay of King's Lynn, close to the Custom House where his father worked. Largely due to the efforts of Brian Howling, an ex-mayor, it was raised in 2000, initially on a temporary support before the preparation of a plinth of Canadian granite in 2001. Holding a telescope and a scrolled map, Vancouver is shown slightly less than lifesize, a youthful figure in 18th century dress, his stance copied from a small statuette in the town's museum. He had sailed twice with Captain Cook before his first voyage to the Pacific coast of North America and Canada to resolve territorial disputes. Returning to the region in 1792, he circumnavigated the island named after him and accurately mapped tens of thousands of landmarks on the winding coastline of British Columbia, in search of an illusory passage to the Atlantic. Vancouver's treatment of native tribes was diplomatic and his regard for his crew ensured their safe return after five years at sea. He died soon after at his home in Surrey.

The sculptor, Penelope Reeve, was born in 1945 and set out as a portrait artist, firstly in Paris, then at Byam Shaw School in London. Continuing as a painter until 1990, she attended Heatherley's Art School and discovered an aptitude for modelling and sculpture. Commissions followed, including statuettes and two half-size elephants for Sezincote House, Gloucestershire, and a 1998 bronze statue of the Earl of Leicester in Holkham Park, which led to her work in King's Lynn.

2000. CAPTAIN GEORGE VANCOUVER BY PENELOPE REEVE KING'S LYNN

For as long as anyone can remember the thick-legged, long-haired figures of Samson and Hercules have been an extra pair of doormen, supporting the porch of the 17th century house which has long served as a dance hall or nightclub. Concern for their conservation led to removal of the original figures in 1994, which were donated to Norfolk Museums Service by the owners of the building. What we see now are fibre-glass replicas with very little detail.

During investigative work at the museum, beneath layer on layer of lead paint, it was decided that Samson, with his lamb and jawbone of an ass, is made of oak and may date from as early as 1660, while Hercules is a late Victorian replacement. Was Samson one of a pair of male caryatids, or figurative supporting pillars, possibly of historical importance? The investigation is still in progress. Even when it is concluded there will remain the question of what to do with the wooden musclemen, conserved or otherwise.

SAMSON & HERCULES
AGE AND ORIGIN UNKNOWN
TOMBLAND, NORWICH

Norfolk is proud of its native hero, but few would compare this Nelson with his monuments in Great Yarmouth or London. The over-lifesize statue of England's naval hero stands in an unrealistic pose near the Cathedral in his home county. The icons are here, the telescope and empty sleeve, though no eye-patch or hat, but the general detail is unfinished. The statue was almost certainly intended for a different viewpoint, probably in competition for raising on a tall pillar, as in London and Dublin. Nelson's face and nose have been eroded, although the marble itself, cleaned this year, is of great durability, having defied every winter since 1854, when it was erected by public subscription in the Market Place, before removal to this site in 1936.

Thomas Milnes, 1813-1888, attended the Academy schools after working under E. H. Baily, the sculptor selected for the statue of Nelson in Trafalgar Square. It is very likely that Norwich's subscribers had hoped for another work by Baily, but they paid Milnes 700 guineas for this statue in 1847, a high fee for a less well-known sculptor. He had some bad luck, having made the first of the lions for Nelson's column in Trafalgar Square; they were rejected and replaced with the huge and famous bronze lions by Edwin Landseer, a painter.

1847. LORD NELSON.
BY THOMAS MILNES
THE CLOSE, NORWICH

A statue of Arthur Wellesley, Duke of Wellington, 1769-1852, stands in Cathedral Close. The 8 feet tall, bronze figure is set on a granite plinth decorated with a medallion of military emblems and the simple inscription, 'WELLINGTON'. It presents the Duke as an older man, holding a lowered sword and with a canon at his feet. The victor at Waterloo rid England of income tax and the threat of Napoleon, for which he was richly rewarded. He lived for another 35 years after the great battle and became a very conservative prime minister and there are many monuments and statues to him, including four grand memorials in London. The one in Norwich was raised by public subscription in 1854 in the Market Place and unveiled before a crowd of 20,000. In 1936 it was relocated close to the Cathedral in order, it is said, to preserve it from possible anti-establishment demonstrations, though this is barely credible and surely masks a planner's stategy.

The sculptor, George Adams, 1821-1898, studied at the R.A schools and then in Rome. He showed three Classical works at the Great Exhibition and was chosen in the following year to take Wellington's death mask. The Norwich statue was his first of four of the Duke, not to mention three others of Wellesley family members. Although the features of Wellington's face are not distinct, the 2nd Duke, once MP for Norwich, wrote to Adams to say that the likeness was, "Considered by myself and those gentlemen who knew him best, as well as by his servants, as the best by far that has appeared".

THE DUKE OF WELLINGTON
BY GEORGE ADAMS, 1854.
THE CLOSE, NORWICH.

To the memory of
THE FOLLOWING OFFICERS AND MEN OF THE NINTH, OR EAST NORFOLK, REGT OF FOOT:
CAP R.J.EDMONDS, LIEUT J.S.CUMMING, 4 SERGEANTS, AND 24 RANK AND FILE,
KILLED, OR MORTALLY WOUNDED, IN THE AFFGHAN CAMPAIGN, 1842,
AT THE KHYBER, MAMMOO-KHAIL, JUGDULLUK, TEZEEN, AND ISTALIF:
AND ALSO OF
MAJOR-GENERAL SIR JOHN M CASKILL, K.C.B.AND K.H.; LIEUT COL A.B.TAYLOR, K.H. AND C.B.
CAP J.DUNNE, CAP J.F.FIELD, LIEUT F.SIEVWRIGHT,
ASSIST SURGEON R.B.GAHAN, 3 SERGT, AND 197 RANK AND FILE,
WHO, WHILE TRIUMPHANTLY OPPOSING THE SIKHS INVADING BRITISH INDIA,
AT MOODKEE, 18 DEC 1845, FEROZESHAH, 21 AND 22 DEC 1845, AND SOBRAON, 10 FEB 1846,
FELL NOBLY ON THE FIELD OF VICTORY, OR WERE THERE MORTALLY WOUNDED,
THIS TABLET IS ERECTED BY THEIR SURVIVING BROTHERS IN ARMS.
"GOD GRANT THEIR SOULS BE AT REST, TO SHARE IN VICTORY OF ENDLESS LIFE!"

Close to the door into the South transept of the Cathedral is an often unnoticed but very beautiful memorial. Backed by slate and set high on the wall, the five foot wide marble tablet is carved in high relief and shows the superb classical figure of Britannia as she kneels in deep mourning over a grave. It was raised to officers and men of the East Norfolk Regiment lost in the first Afghan War, 1839-1842, culminating in the total destruction of British forces in the Khyber passes. Added to the inscription are the names of those who fell during the first Sikh War, 1845. With hindsight we view England's Imperial history, as the names of battles – Jugdullur, Moodkee – are conjured in a foreign tongue.

E. H. Baily, 1788-1867, was an extremely able sculptor. As a boy, even before attending the Academy Schools, he showed such talent that he was summoned to assist the sculptor and illustrator John Flaxman. During his career he made many great monuments, including works in Parliament, Buckingham Palace and the facade of the National Gallery, as well as the 17 ton statue of Nelson high above Trafalgar Square. The Afghan Campaign tablet, one of the earliest war memorials, is his only work in Norfolk.

1848. AFGHAN CAMPAIGN MEMORIAL
BY E. H. BAILY, R.A
NORWICH CATHEDRAL

The 12 feet tall granite obelisk with its drinking fountain in Tombland marks the spot where there was once a well and machinery for gathering water for higher parts of the city. Its shape stands out against a view of the tapering Cathedral spire in the background. The drinking fountain no longer flows. It was raised by the Gurney family at the suggestion of John Bell, who was busy putting up a much larger obelisk to commemorate the Quaker philanthropist, Samuel Gurney, at Stratford, on the edge of London. Immovable, anciently classical and somehow mysterious, obelisks appear all over England. Not far away, in Rosary Road, thirty of them cluster on a wooded hillside in the old cemetery.

The Norfolk-born sculptor, John Bell, 1811-1895, was very successful in London. At the time he was engaged in the Crimean War Memorial and the Albert Memorial, for which he made the first proposal as an obelisk. He lectured the Society of Art about obelisks, drinking fountains and the art-treatment of polished granite. His works in Norwich include 'Armed Science', (-see overleaf), the Crome Memorial, and 'The Babes in the Wood', in marble, presented by his daughter to Norwich Castle Museum.

1861. GURNEY OBELISK & DRINKING
FOUNTAIN,
SUGGESTED BY JOHN BELL
TOMBLAND, NORWICH

Conservation alert for the frost-eaten face of the beautiful statue at the Soldiers' Memorial in Norwich. This is the unique Doulton terracotta version of John Bell's 1855 Royal Academy exhibit, 'Armed Science', first commissioned in marble by Lord Waveney for Woolwich Artillery. The 8 feet tall female figure stands, with demi-armour and helmet, in a reflective pose, holding a sponge or rammer for cannonry. Known to some as 'The Spirit of the Army', the soft red and buff statue is sited on an inscribed pediment in the City Cemetry, by Dereham Road. It was presented by seven Norfolk gentlemen in October 1878.

Born in Norfolk, the sculptor, John Bell, followed a career in London, with grand commissions and introductions to manufacturers. For the 1876 U.S centenary, Henry Doulton cast a copy of the huge sculpture Bell had made for the Albert Memorial, which survived only 55 years in Chicago, destroyed by the icy East wind. 'Armed Science' was cast in the same terracotta. Norfolk too has a biting easterly and the erosion on the windward side of the statue's face is advanced. Before long, without repair or removal, she will be lost. So how does the conservation process get started?

1878 'ARMED SCIENCE',
DOULTON TERRACOTTA BY JOHN BELL
SOLDIERS' MEMORIAL, NORWICH

Just inside the roadside grounds of the present Norfolk & Norwich Hospital is a bronze half-size Mother and Child. Modelled in the classical fashion, the mother's diaphanous gown is but a hint in metal and the child is a tough male cherub. This was purchased with £1,000 left in the will of Sir John Boileau of Ketteringham for such a purpose, and was instated with a drinking fountain beneath a small brick-towered structure at the nearby junction of Newmarket Road and Ipswich Road.

With the onslaught of motorised traffic, the structure was taken down and the bronze group was placed across the road in the N&N grounds. Boileau was a committee member of the Royal Society of Art and would have met the sculptor, Sir Joseph Boehm, 1834-1890, who made many works in the Royal Collection. But what will happen to this sculpture, the remains of the squire of Ketteringham's gift to Norwich, when the hospital moves out of the city to the new site?

§ *see notes page 46*

1874. 'MOTHER & CHILD' BY SIR J. BOEHM NORFOLK & NORWICH HOSPITAL.

There are three marble memorials in the Cathedral's North transept. The most luxurious is that of John Pelham, 65th Bishop of Norwich from 1857 to 1893. When he died a year later, at the age of 82, a public subscription was opened for a memorial, completed in 1896. Dressed in clerical robes, old Pelham's highly polished figure is stretched out, but one's eye is drawn to the large base he lies upon, which is very ornate, made of red marble and inscribed with brass lettering.

The commission was taken by the sculptor, James Nesfield Forsyth, who had already established a practice of providing similar monuments. Born in 1841, the son of an architect and sculptor, he had studied at the Academy schools and in Paris and made memorials for bishops in Bristol and Manchester Cathedrals. His sculpture in Norwich is in direct contrast with the neighbouring seated statue of Bishop Bathurst, which has no details or extras. Made in 1841, it was a late work by Sir Francis Chantrey, who, in the same year, made at least eight other statues and died, a rich man.

1896. J. T. PELHAM,
65TH BISHOP OF NORWICH
BY JAMES NESFIELD FORSYTH,
NORWICH CATHEDRAL

A tall monument surmounted by a sword-bearing, winged female towers above Agricultural Plain and can be seen from afar down Prince of Wales Road. This is 'Victory', a beautiful bronze figure, her improbable and stylised wings raised above her head, known to some as "Peace", to others, "The Angel of Death". At each corner of the large Portland stone plinth, ionic columns frame bronze shields inscribed with the names of 300 Norfolk soldiers lost in the Boer War. The plinth alone, with its granite base, cost £1,600, a large sum at the time. The memorial was erected in 1904 by General Wynn and received conservation in 1988. Significantly, the adjacent Shire Hall now houses the Norfolk Regimental Museum.

The winged figure of Victory was made by George Wade, 1853-1933. Originally a barrister, he was a self-taught sculptor, who exhibited at the Academy and became friendly with Sir E. Boehm whose studio he took over in 1890. Wade specialised in bronze statuettes, of either royal or military subjects. He made public monuments to Edward VII in Bootle, Reading and Whitechapel and his 1908 statue to Queen Alexandria stands in the courtyard of the London Hospital. While making the Norwich memorial, he was assisted by his brother, Fairfax Wade.

1904. 'VICTORY', BOER WAR
MEMORIAL
BY G. E WADE
AGRICULTURAL PLAIN, NORWICH

There are two stone figures set in niches on either side of the Palladian front of Surrey House, Norwich Union's 1904 mansion-office. The statue to the right is of Sir Samuel Bignold, 1791-1875, son of the founder and secretary of the insurance business from 1815 onwards. He was also Norwich's mayor in the 1850's and is shown in official robes. The other figure is that of William Talbot, Bishop of Oxford, leader of an incorporated Amicable Society, lending an air of ecclesiastical respectability to the enterprise. Larger than lifesize, both statues appear older than they actually are, in keeping with the magnificent building, designed by the esteemed Norwich architect, George Skipper. Just inside is a truly spectacular hall, decorated in ten coloured marbles from a cargo intended for Westminster Cathedral and by the front door are bronze reliefs of 'Solace' and 'Protection' by S. Young, who also signs the unique bronze lamps outside.

The statues were carved in Portland stone at London workshops by Leon-Joseph Chavalliaud, 1858-1921, a French sculptor who specialised in portrait busts. Around the turn of the century he received a number of English commissions, including the celebrated 1897 statue of the actress Sarah Siddons as Lady Macbeth at Paddington and that of Cardinal Newman at Brompton Oratory, set in a niche and quite similar to the Norwich Union pair.

SIR SAMUEL BIGNOLD
BY L. CHAVALLIAUD, 1904
SURREY HOUSE, NORWICH

The tricentenary of the birth of Sir Thomas Browne, (1605-1682), is remembered in a statue on Hay Hill, opposite the house where he practised as a physician and close to his grave at St. Peter's Mancroft. Browne was born in London and travelled in Ireland and studied in Italy before settling in Norwich. During the Civil War he remained a royalist, and was knighted by King Charles II on a visit to Norwich in 1671. Browne was author of 'Religio Medici' and the later 'Hydrotaphia'- a book about urn burials. Beneath the seated scholar's memorial, the plinth itself is shaped like a squared urn. He is shown as a meditative figure in period dress, seated upon a curved and heavy chair. Elbow on knee, hand on brow, he contemplates the shard of a broken urn he holds in his right hand. This is where a beer bottle is often placed or a pigeon sits.

The sculptor, Henry Pegram, 1862-1937, started his career as assistant to H. Thornycroft. He specialised in portrait busts, usually of classical subjects. At the time of 'New' sculpture, he had shown symbolism in the ethereal figures of 'Ignis Fatuus', a bronze relief, now in Cardiff Museum. The same technique was used for figurative panels of Brittannia and 'Industry' for London's Imperial Institute. Pegram was at the height of his powers when he modelled Thomas Browne in 1905.

28.
1905. SIR THOMAS BROWNE
BY HENRY PEGRAM
HAY HILL, NORWICH.

The bronze bust of Edith Cavell stares bravely ahead, above a white stone plinth and a lone rifleman, conferring wreaths of honour. Inscribed 'Nurse, Patriot and Martyr', the memorial stands by the outer wall of the Cathedral. Edith Cavell was born in 1865 at Swardeston, 4 miles from the city, and chose to be a nurse. Remaining in Brussels after the German occupation of Belgium, she tended the wounded of both sides. In 1915, after she had assisted 200 allied soldiers to escape to neutral Holland, she was executed by firing squad. Her body was removed from its temporary grave and brought home, to be buried beyond the Cathedral's East end. The monument was originally sited in the roadway nearby, in front of the Maids Head Hotel, where it was unveiled by Queen Alexandria in 1918. It was later moved to its present site in order to allow more traffic.

The sculptor Henry Pegram, 1862-1937, had already completed, some years earlier, the excellent Norwich statue of Sir Thomas Browne and this surely influenced his selection for the Cavell monument. At first sight, the combination of Edith Cavell's bronze head above the stone rifleman and bayonet seems a confusing mismatch. This is often said of certain war memorials, where different concepts are put together. Pegram later made the Cunard War Memorial in Liverpool.

**1918. Monument to Edith Cavell
by Henry Pegram
Tombland, Norwich**

1936. HERALDIC LIONS
BY ALFRED HARDIMAN
CITY HALL, NORWICH

The Heraldic Lions on either side of the steps in front of City Hall are magnificent. With lashing tails, patterned manes and gaping jaws, they stand like guardians before what Pevsner descibed as the foremost interwar public building in England. The two City Hall architects, C. James and S. Rowland, visited the British Empire Exhibition of 1936. Seeing a single 8 feet long bronze lion, they purchased it from the sculptor and commissioned the casting of its twin in time for the opening of the building by the King and Queen in October 1938. In due course the emblem on the city council's stationery was adapted to resemble the sculptured pair.

The sculptor, Alfred Hardiman, 1891-1949, went to the Royal College of Art and studied at the British School in Rome. He won the RBS medal in 1939, and was later elected R.A. Hardiman made bas-reliefs and took commissions for small memorials, though he is best known for the statue of Earl Haig in London's Whitehall.

1956. 'Reclining Figure', by Henry Moore, Outside Sainsbury Centre for Visual Arts, U.E.A, Norwich

'Reclining Figure' is an 8 ft long bronze shape of roughly human proportions, with a barely recognisable head and no hands or feet. Leaning on one elbow upon a heavy dark plinth, it is sited close to the entrance of the Sainsbury Centre for Visual Arts and is seen before the open park landscape surrounding the University of East Anglia. Originally modelled in 1956, a small plaque explains that this was the 4th cast of 8, acquired in 1962 and brought here in 1985. The sculptor's name explains all.

It would be impossible to overestimate the status of Henry Moore, 1898-1986. With a sixty year career and success in his lifetime, his is one of the most renowned names in 20th century sculpture. The region is fortunate to have a few of his works, part of the generous gift of the late Sir Robert and Lady Sainsbury Collection, later housed in the celebrated gallery and centre. 'Reclining Figure' and two other bronzes are outside; those inside include 'Mother & Child', carved in green ironstone, bought for £158 in 1933, and now priceless. Henry Moore was a Yorkshireman, but his parents moved to Wighton and he had lasting associations with Norfolk. Anyone from this area will recognise the shapes of pebbles and flints seen in some of his works.

The path in the old moated gardens beneath the Castle leads past a bronze sculpture called 'Sea Form'. Semi-abstract and yet mask-like in metal, it has the appearance of a punctured stone megalith. The 6 ft tall dented slab is made transparent by different sized holes or gaps to the landscape beyond. Purchased by Norfolk Museums with grants from the Victoria & Albert Museum and the Gulbenkian Foundation, this is the third in a series of six sculptures linked to the distant landscape of Cornwall and recalls the ancient stone uprights of western Britain. The sculptor had written a letter stating, "I was prompted by the sort of associative urge which is overwhelming on these rocky hilltops to engrave or seek out the secret sign which releases the life of a form at the focal point".

Barbara Hepworth, 1903-1975, studied at Leeds and the Royal College of Art with Henry Moore in the 1920s and won a year long scholarship in Italy. Initially with stone figures and animals and later with abstracts, she gradually gained an international reputation. Her 'Single Form' was instated in 1963 outside the UN building in New York. She loved Cornwall and spent the later part of her life there with her second husband, the sculptor Ben Nicholson. Tragically, she died when her St. Ives studio caught fire.

1964. SEA FORM (ATLANTIC)
BY BARBARA HEPWORTH
CASTLE GARDENS, NORWICH

1969. 'UNTITLED'
BY BERNARD MEADOWS
PROSPECT HOUSE, ECN, NORWICH

The untitled, massive, abstract composition that fronts the Eastern Counties Newspapers' building is very much at home after more than thirty years in the city. The sculptor, Bernard Meadows, knew Norwich and the gilt sign of the Woolpack Inn in nearby Golden Ball Street, a tightly packed sack, provided him with the idea of compression. This is expressed in the squashed and dimpled bronze shapes, above which the large gleaming ball, a symbol of optimism, reflects the sky. The entire work, twenty feet long, is attached to the building with large white granite blocks and a wall of round flints, since echoed in parts of the outside of nearby Castle Mall.

The sculptor Bernard Meadows was born in Norwich in 1915 and attended Norwich Art School, where he was introduced to Henry Moore and worked as his assistant for four years before successfully venturing on his own. In addition to smaller, surreal models of birds and insects, the artist's larger works front other buildings, including Hertfordshire County Hall and the Trade Union building in London. Meadows took pleasure in the making of 'Untitled' on the front of the new ECN building in 1969. At the time he was Professor of Sculpture at the Royal College of Art , with exhibits in galleries throughout the world.

1982. 'EXTRAPOLATION',
BY LILIANE LIJN,
U.E.A, NORWICH

From certain angles, 'Extrapolation', with its 33 triangular layers, is almost solid, then it is transparent, its body made of air. Fabricated in a leaning complex of thin stainless-steel strips, it expresses the optical effect of a central prism. For many people the construction holds memories of the courtyard of the Norwich Library, for which it was designed and originally sited in 1982, a focal point against the glass and concrete of that building. It was moved a few months before the notorious fire which destroyed the library in 1994. First commissioned by Norfolk Contemporary Art Society after a public vote in competition with other sculptors' designs, 'Extrapolation' is now relocated at the university, outside another library, by agreement with Norfolk County Council and the sculptor.

Liliane Lijn was born in 1939 in New York and came to Europe at the age of 18, leaving Art History studies in Paris to draw and experiment in three dimensions. She settled in England in 1966, by which time her work was characterised by new approaches to light and movement and the use of modern materials. Her 'Circle of Light' was an important commission in Milton Keynes. She was a pioneer of Kinetic Art, exhibiting at the Serpentine Gallery in 1976 and the Hayward in 2000. The building of Norwich's new library is an opportunity for new public sculpture, to be announced at the eleventh hour, but 'Extrapolation' will stay where it is. It catches wind and light in a way it never could before.

The Wader is in the Hotel Nelson gardens and can be seen across the river from Norwich Station. A lifesize bronze figure of a female, she wades in a shallow pool, as if in slow motion. One hand keeps her dress dry, the other carries her shoes. Looking into the water and hidden behind the brim of her round hat, she is unaware of being seen. Evocative of Summer, this is a pleasing image, especially in conjunction with the pool and waterfall. It was installed in 1987, the first of a few contemporary works to be sited in the garden, a little sculpture park in itself, by the hotel's owners, who manage a policy of spending a percentage of profit on art works.

Colin Miller, born in 1943, is the son of the painter and portraitist, Bunty Miller. He turned to sculpture in the 1960s, first exhibiting at the Royal Academy in 1973 and then spent a decade on the island of Paros, working in marble and olive wood. Returning to Norfolk, he modelled Wader in 1986, followed by pieces in private collections and later public commissions in London and Norwich, including 'Gaia' on Surrey Street. With a major exhibition in London in 2001, Miller describes his work generally as both figurative and abstract, inspired by natural forms and Greek mythology.

**1986. THE WADER
BY COLIN MILLER
HOTEL NELSON, NORWICH**

'Monument to Daedalus' is sited on Castle Green, or, less romantically, on the shopping mall car park roof. Seen from afar, it has considerable presence and some menace, like a 7ft bird-scarer, or a traffic camera, overlooking the melee of the city centre. Up close, like a warrior's suit of armour waiting to be worn, it is a large, sand-cast aluminium helmet on a steel post, with a pair of speed-angled wings bolted on. Is it a representation or an afterthought of the mythic aeronaut? Reading the inscription, 'Through man's endeavour his spirit lives on into the future', one could forget about Daedalus's son, Icarus, who exceeded the limits of his father's technology and crashed to earth.

This is by Jonathan Clarke, who was born in 1961 and worked under his sculptor father before exhibiting in Britain and Europe from 1989 onwards. The piece, reminiscent of 'Robocop', and others by him, are noted as hidden, inner beings, covered by protective armour. It was first exhibited in 1993, and acquired by the Norfolk Contemporary Art Society for raising on Castle Green in 1998. Laudably, this site is especially intended for sculptures. Apart from an attractive bronze Parrot Head by the Norfolk sculptor, Bernard Reynolds, 'Daedalus' so far stands alone, a science fiction cyborg in the middle of Norwich's changing landscape.

1993. 'Monument to Daedalus'
by Jonathan Clarke.
Castle Green, Norwich

NOTES

*9. NOTE: There is some controversy between interpretations based on what was intended (as shown in 'Coke of Norfolk and his Friends', by A. Stirling, 1909) and what was actually portrayed in stone. With a view to the artistic composition of the entire relief, the sculptor evidently adjusted the designs and positions of figures. For drawing my attention to these differences and for valuable information, I am grateful to both to Mrs. C. Hiskey, MA, Dip Arch, Holkham Archivist, and Mrs. S Wade-Martins, Phd, Honorary Research fellow, Centre for East Anglian studies, UEA, and author of 'A great estate at work, the Holkham estate and its inhabitants in the nineteenth century' (C.U.P. 1980).

*14-NOTE:After this feature was printed, a reader from Norwich wrote to the editor, in defence of 'the bright star of liberty'. Pointing out that Paine proposed a welfare state paid for out of taxation, pensions for people over 50, child benefit, free hostels for the homeless and funeral allowances for the poor, the correspondent John Garrett, former MP for Norwich South, stated, "No Norfolk man has been such an influence for good".

*24. NOTE:After this feature was printed, The Eastern Daily Press received a letter from Mr P. J Cooper of Norwich, who had been part of the N&N Hosptal Management Committee in 1968 when it was offered the sculpture, (by whom he did not state). He urged that the statue should now stay where it was, an aspect of Victorian Norwich, although the hospital is to be dismantled to make way for housing.

BIBLIOGRAPHY

A Dictionary of Sculptors in Bronze. James Mackay. 1977, Antique Collector's Club.
A History of Ditchingham. Rev John Charles Scudamore M.A
A History of Norwich. Frank Meeres. 1998, Phillmore.
Coke of Norfolk & his Friends. A.M.W. Stirling, John Lane / Bodley Head. 1912 edition
Dictionary of British Sculptors 1660-1851. Rupert Gunniss. The Abbey Library, 1951.
East Anglian Village & Town Signs. Ursula Bourne, 1986.
Henry Bell. Alderman & Architect. E. Beloe / Lynn Advertiser 3rd February 1894.
John Bell – The Sculptor's Life and Works. R.Barnes. Frontier Publishing,1999.
Sculptured Monuments in Norfolk Churches. Noel Spencer. 1977 Norfolk Churches Trust.
The Buildings of England: Norwich & North Norfolk. N. Pevsner & B.Wilson. Penguin,
The Maharajah's Box.C.Campbell, HarperCollins,2001
The Monument Guide to England & Wales. Jo Darke. MacDonald & Co, 1991.
The Popular Guide to Norfolk Churches. D.Mortlock & C.V.Roberts. 1985 Acorn Editns.
Public Sculpture – A User's Guide.English Heritage, 2000.
The Recreations of a Norfolk Antiquary. Walter Rye, 1920

ACKNOWLEDGEMENTS

The author wishes to acknowledge the generous assistance of individuals and organisations towards the publication. Before all is the debt of thanks to Peter Franzen, Managing Editor of The Eastern Daily Press, for the encouragement to commence the features which make up this book. Also to Ian Bullock, Features Editor, who oversaw the initial production of the features in the Spotlight on Sculpture series in the newspaper, and to Dennis Whitehead and the press photographers, Denise Bradley, Graham Corney, Simon Finlay, John Hocknell, Bill Smith and Keiron Tovell (EDP photos on pages 9, 10, 11, 12, 14, 16, 21, 22, 27, 28, 30, 31, 33, 34, 37, 38, 41, 42, 44 and 45). Thanks also to Magdalen Russell, Norfolk County Literature Officer, for her enthusiasm for the publication and proofing the final manuscript.

For information and assistance with research, the author wishes to thank Anne Den Engelsea, National Trust, Blickling; John Maddison of Ely; Christine Hiskey, Holkham Archives; Nicholas Hills and Andrew Edmondson of Tittleshall; Cmdr & Mrs. Cheyne, Ditchingham; Brian Howling, Dr Paul Richard and Anne Roberts of King's Lynn Civic Society; Kings Lynn Reference Library; Mrs P. Mlejnecky, Berghapton; Mrs C.Ebbage, Great Yarmouth; Mr Bushnell, Gt Yarmouth Borough Council; Mrs S.Wade Martins, Centre for East Anglian Studies; Susan Maddock, Principal Archivist, Norfolk Record Office; Robert Short, Norfolk Contemporary Art Society; Mr Harbinder Singh, Walsall; Norma Watt, Castle Museum, Norwich.

Finally, for arrangements for funding to meet production costs, the publishers gratefully acknowledge the work of Mari Martin, Mary Muir and Julie Hewitt in administration of Norfolk County Council Visual Arts Fund, and for the representation of this publication to Norwich City Council Special Projects Fund by Mr V.Aston, the Council's Arts and Culture officer.

INDEX